PACIFIC COAST HORNS

Bugler's Holiday

B♭ TRUMPET

MUSIC MINUS ONE

6828

SUGGESTIONS FOR USING THIS MMO EDITION

We have tried to create a product that will provide you an easy way to learn and perform these compositions with a full ensemble in the comfort of your own home. The following MMO features and techniques will help you maximize the effectiveness of the MMO practice and performance system:

Because it involves a fixed accompaniment performance, there is an inherent lack of flexibility in tempo. We have observed generally accepted tempi, and always in the originally intended key, but some may wish to perform at a different tempo, or to slow down or speed up the accompaniment for practice purposes; or to alter the piece to a more comfortable key. For maximum flexibility, you can purchase from MMO specialized CD players & recorders which allow variable speed while maintaining proper pitch, and vice versa. This is an indispensable tool for the serious musician and you may wish to look into purchasing this useful piece of equipment for full enjoyment of all your MMO editions.

We want to provide you with the most useful practice and performance accompaniments possible. If you have any suggestions for improving the MMO system, please feel free to contact us. You can reach us by e-mail at *info@musicminusone.com*.

6828

CONTENTS

ISBN 1-59615-782-8

Bugler's Holiday

Trumpet 1 in B-flat

LEROY ANDERSON
arr. by P. CHAUVIN

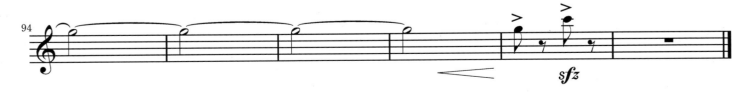

The Barber of Seville Overture

Trumpet 1

Gioacchino Rossini
Arr. by Charles Warren

Trumpet 1

In the Dark

Bix Beiderbecke
Arr. Charles Warren

MMO 6828

Big Band Montage II

Trumpet 1 in B-flat + Flugelhorn

Woodchopper's Ball, Cherry Pink and Apple Blossom White,
Begin the Beguine, Opus One, Dream

arr. by P. CHAUVIN

(Cherry Pink and Apple Blossom White)

D Medium Cha-Cha ♩ = 124

(Begin the Beguine)

V.S.

MMO 6828

Begin The Beguine (from "Jubilee")
Words and Music by COLE PORTER
©1935 (Renewed) WB MUSIC CORP.
All Rights Reserved. Used by Permission.

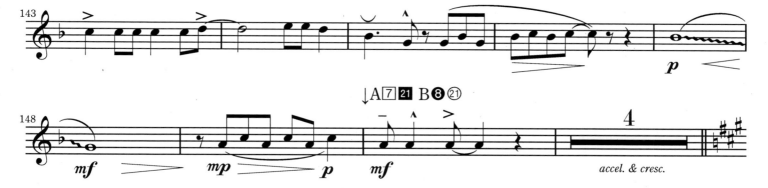

V.S.

Opus One
written by Sy Oliver
Copyright ©1943 (Renewed) by Embassy Music Corporation (BMI)
International Copyright Secured. All Rights Reserved. Reprinted by Permission.

MMO 6828

13

Dream
Words and Music by JOHNNY MERCER

I Wanna Be Like You

Trumpet 1

Words and Music by
Richard M. Sherman and Robert B. Sherman

D. S. al Coda

Operatic Rag

Trumpet 1

Julius Lenzberg - Charles Warren

MMO 6828

Take Five

Trumpet 1

Paul Desmond
arr. by P. CHAUVIN

Flower Duet

From "Lakme"

Trumpet 1

Leo Delibes
Arranged by Charles Warren

When the Saints Go Marching In

Trumpet 1

Traditional

MUSIC MINUS ONE
50 Executive Boulevard
Elmsford, New York 10523-1325
1.800.669.7464 (U.S.)/914.592.1188 (International)

www.musicminusone.com
e-mail: mmogroup@musicminusone.com

MMO 6828

Pub. No. 00895

Printed in Canada